Bake Sales and Birthday Parties

A
Collection
Of Special Treats

Jackie Gannaway

Published in Austin, TX by COOKBOOK CUPBOARD, P.O. Box 50053, Austin, TX 78763 (512) 477-7070

ISBN 1-885597-12-6

Artwork by Mosey 'N Me   1436 Baird   Katy, Texas 77493   (713) 391-2281

Jackie Gannaway

Mail Order Information

Cookbook Cupboard sells mini cookie cutters in a variety of shapes as well as plastic molds for shaping Crispy Treats. If you are interested, send a note to the address below asking for an order blank.

To order a copy of this book send a check for $3.95 + $1.50 for shipping per order (TX residents add 8 % sales tax) to Cookbook Cupboard, P.O. Box 50053, Austin, TX 78763. Send a note asking for this title by name.

I f you would like a descriptive list of all the fun titles in The Kitchen Crafts Collection, send a note asking for an order blank.

Other books of interest might be: "Cookie Cutter Crafts", " Holiday Cookie Cutter Crafts", "Cake in a Jar", "Gift Goodies".

All the Kitchen Crafts titles are $3.95. Shipping is $1.50 per order up to $30.00.

Bake Sales and Birthday Parties

Do you need ideas for school party treats, bake sales, fund raising carnivals, concession stands at the little league games, church bazaars, birthday parties?

This book is full of ideas for single serving treats as well as ideas on how to wrap them!

For a complete list of all the recipes please look in the index on page 32.

Birthday Party Fun

♥ Put balloons all around the room before the birthday child wakes up.

♥ Use a sheet of butcher paper for a tablecloth. Let kids all decorate it (and sign it) with crayons or markers. You roll it up, date it and save it. Protect table underneath from markers coming through. Can also use a white tablecloth or a sheet.

♥ Stack 2 or 3 Lifesavers candies as holders for birthday candles on cake or cupcakes.

♥ Bake an unwrapped round peppermint candy inside a cupcake. The child who gets it wins a prize.

♥ Put tiny favors or money inside balloons and blow up balloons.

♥ Tie helium balloons in the hole in a Bundt cake.

♥ Give each child a cupcake with a candle so they all get a candle to blow out.

♥ Give each child a white frosted cupcake. Have tubes of each color squirt frosting available and let them decorate their own cupcake.

♥ Let the birthday child decorate a plain white frosted sheet cake with squirt frosting.

♥ Blow up a balloon. Write party information on balloon with a marking pen. Deflate balloon and send as an invitation.

3

Ice Cream Cone Cakes

1 cake mix
2 eggs
1 (21 oz.) can pie filling

18 large or 30 small flat
bottom ice cream cones
1 can frosting

1. Place dry cake mix, eggs and pie filling in large bowl and mix with electric mixer until well blended.
2. Fill each cone 3/4 full of cake batter. Place on baking sheet and bake according to cake mix directions for cupcakes. Test for doneness with a toothpick. Cool 20 minutes.
3. Frost cooled cone cakes. Decorate as desired. Serves 18.

TRY THESE FLAVORS:
Yellow cake and peach pie filling,
Chocolate cake and cherry pie filling,
Lemon cake and cherry pie filling,
Strawberry cake and strawberry pie filling,
Peach cake and apricot pie filling

These can also be baked in cake pans or muffin pans. Bake at 350 for the time listed on the cake mix. These are good simple, 3-ingredient cakes.

FOR A CHANGE: Cone Cakes can be made with a regular cake mix. Fill cone 3/4 full of batter. Follow cake mix directions on cake mix box for baking. Test for doneness with a toothpick. Cool 20 minutes before icing.

♥ BAKE SALES: These are hard to wrap because of the shape and the frosting. They can be sold at a concession stand by standing them upright in muffin tins.

♥ BIRTHDAY PARTIES: Place an individual candle in each one and let each child blow out his candle. Let kids frost and decorate these. Fun to serve cake in a cone and ice cream in a dish.

Sharks in the Sea

1 (4-serving size) pkg.
   blue Jello
1 (4-serving size) pkg.
   lemon Jello
water to mix Jello

gummi sharks or fish
   (available in mall
   candy stores)
6 (9 oz.) clear plastic cups

1. Combine both flavors Jello and mix according to package directions. Divide gelatin among 6 clear plastic cups. Refrigerate until slightly thickened.
2. Place some candy fish into each cup.
3. Refrigerate until thickened.

♥ BAKE SALES: Could be sold at a concession stand where there is refrigeration.

♥ BIRTHDAY PARTIES: A fun snack and not as rich as some birthday party treats.

Chocolate Dipped Ice Cream Cones

1. Dip the edge of an ice cream cone in melted chocolate. Sprinkle with colored sprinkles.
2. Place in refrigerator until set. (Can stand in glasses or in a muffin tin while setting.)
3. After the chocolate sets up, these can be kept at room temperature until serving.

♥ BAKE SALES: Sell these cones in packages of 6 in a white box lined with colorful tissue paper. Sell ice cream in these cones at concession stands.

♥ BIRTHDAY PARTIES: Prepare these ahead and serve ice cream at the party in them.

Peanut Butter Popcorn Balls

1/4 cup packed brown sugar   1/8 tsp. salt
1/4 cup light corn syrup   4 cups popped corn
2 Tb. creamy peanut butter   1/2 cup salted peanuts

1. Mix first 4 ingredients in microsafe dish. Micro on high 1 1/2 minutes.
2. Mix popcorn and peanuts in large bowl.
3. Pour hot mixture over popcorn. Mix well.
4. Cool slightly and shape into balls. (Dip your hands in water for easier shaping.)

Rocky Road Popcorn Balls

3 1/2 quarts popped corn   1 cup marshmallow creme
2 cups sugar   1 cup semisweet chocolate chip
1 cup evaporated milk   1 tsp. vanilla
1/4 cup margarine

1. Place popcorn in large bowl. Set aside.
2. Combine sugar, milk and margarine in heavy pan. Cook over medium heat, stirring constantly until sugar dissolves and mixture comes to a boil. Boil 5 minutes, stirring occasionally. Remove from heat.
3. Add remaining ingredients to hot mixture. Stir until chocolate chips are melted.
4. Pour over popcorn, stirring until completely coated.
5. Cool slightly and shape into balls. (Dip your hands in water for easier shaping.) Chill until firm.

♥ WRAPPING: Wrap popcorn balls in plastic wrap (or sandwich bags) or colored cellophane and tie with multi-colored curling ribbons. Can add a craft stick as a handle.

♥ BAKE SALES: These are good for Halloween carnivals and concession stands.

Pastel Popcorn Balls

2 1/2 quarts popped corn
1/2 cup corn syrup
1/3 cup water
1 cup sugar
1/2 tsp. salt

1/4 cup butter or mar-
    garine cut in pieces
1 tsp. vanilla
food coloring

1. Place popcorn in large bowl. Set aside.
2. Combine corn syrup, water, sugar and salt in heavy pan. Cook over medium heat, stirring constantly, until sugar dissolves and mixture comes to a boil.
3. Cook to 255° on a candy thermometer (hard ball stage).
4. Remove from heat. Stir in butter and vanilla.
5. Add food coloring, a few drops at a time, until desired color is obtained.
6. Immediately pour over popped corn, stirring until completely coated.
7. Cool slightly and shape into balls. (Dip your hands in water for easier shaping.)

Popcorn Ball Jack-O-Lanterns

Use recipe above, using red and yellow food coloring to tint mixture orange. Shape into balls. Use black string licorice for a mouth and candy corn for nose and mouth. Wrap and tie with orange and black curling ribbons.

♥ WRAPPING: Wrap popcorn balls in plastic wrap (or sandwich bags) or colored cellophane and tie with multi-colored curling ribbons. Can add a craft stick as a handle.

♥ BAKE SALES: These are good for Halloween carnivals and concession stands.

7

Popcorn Happy Faces

Use recipe for Pastel Popcorn Balls on pg. 7, tinting yellow. Shape into 4" round, 1 1/2" thick circles. Use squirt frosting to make happy faces on circle. Insert a craft stick into bottom. Wrap in plastic wrap and tie with colored curling ribbons..

Popcorn Cake

6 quarts popped corn	1 tsp. vanilla
1 cup margarine	1 cup peanuts
1/2 cup light corn syrup	1 cup M and M's candies
2 cups firmly packed	1 cup small gum drops
brown sugar	assorted candies for decoration

1. Place popcorn in very large bowl. Grease a two piece tube pan.
2. In a heavy pan, combine margarine, corn syrup and brown sugar. Cook over medium heat and stir with a wooden spoon until it comes to a boil. Boil 1 minute.
3. Remove from heat and stir in vanilla.
4. Pour hot mixture over popcorn and stir until well coated. Cool slightly and add peanuts and candies.
5. Pack into tube pan. Cover lightly and cool at room temperature overnight.
6. Remove from pan (use a plain table knife to loosen from pan). Place on serving plate. Decorate with assorted candies and squirt frosting.

♥ WRAPPING: Wrap popcorn cake in clear plastic wrap with a big bow on top and a colorful tag that tells what it is.

♥ BAKE SALES: Wrap as described above. It will be a very unusual item for a bake sale.

♥ BIRTHDAY PARTIES: Can tie a bunch of helium balloons through the hole in the middle of the tube cake.

8

Puppy Chow for People

1 stick margarine
1/2 cup peanut butter
1 (12 oz.) pkg. semisweet
   chocolate chips

1 (12.3 oz.) box Crispix
   cereal
3 cups powdered sugar

1. Melt margarine, peanut butter and chocolate chips in double boiler.
2. Place cereal in large bowl and pour melted mixture over, mixing carefully.
3. Place powdered sugar into large brown paper bag and add cereal mixture a little at a time.
4. Shake bag to coat cereal with powdered sugar.

This is a sweet snack. It resembles puppy chow.

♥ WRAPPING: Place in a large plastic dog dish (new!) and wrap in clear plastic wrap. Can also be placed in sandwich bags and tied with ribbons. Add a tag that says "Puppy Chow for People" and has a picture of a dog.

♥ BAKE SALES: Sell wrapped one of the ways above for a different, fun, bake sale item.

♥ BIRTHDAY PARTIES: Serve a large dog dish or give favors of little baggies. Good for parties featuring a puppy theme.

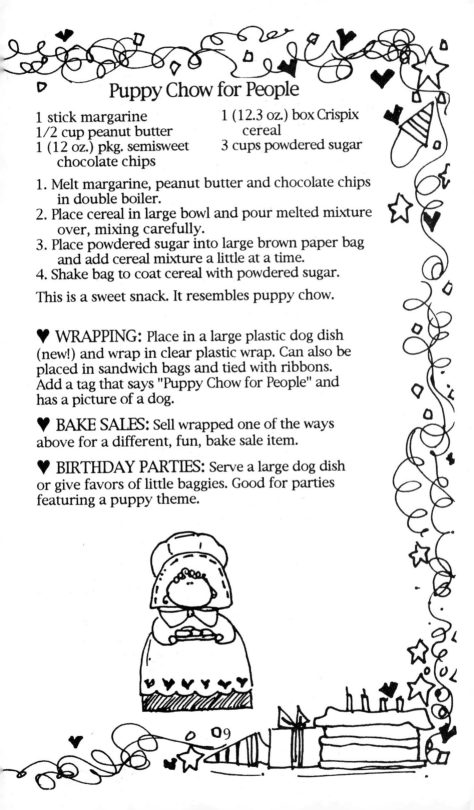

Individual Cheesecakes

12 vanilla wafers
2 (8 oz.) blocks cream
    cheese
1/2 cup sugar

1 tsp. vanilla
2 eggs
canned pie filling,
    chilled
foil cupcake liners

1. Line muffin tins with foil liners. Place one
    vanilla wafer in each liner.
2. Place cream cheese, sugar and vanilla in large
    bowl and mix with electric mixer until well
    blended. Add eggs and mix until well blended.
3. Pour cheesecake mixture over vanilla wafers,
    filling liner 3/4 full.
4. Bake at 325 for 25 minutes.
5. Cool in pan, then chill in refrigerator.
6. Top with chilled cherry or blueberry pie filling.

♥ BAKE SALES: These are good packaged in
boxes of 6 for a bake sale, or sold individually
at concession stands.

♥ BIRTHDAY PARTIES: Good for adults served in
a dessert assortment. Make some cherry and some
blueberry for a Fourth of July party.

Flowerpot Cake and Ice Cream

1. Line very small clay flowerpots with heavy duty
    foil. Spray foil with cooking spray.
2. Put 1/2 cup cake batter in each flowerpot.
3. Bake at 350 for 20 to 25 minutes. Test for doneness
    with a toothpick. Cool.
4. Top with a scoop of ice cream. Cover ice cream
    with crushed chocolate cookies to resemble dirt.
    Wrap in foil and freeze up to 24 hours.
5. At serving time decorate with gummi worms
    or stick in a drinking straw and insert a
        flower into straw.

Dirt Cups

2 cups milk
1 (4 serving size) box choc-
    olate instant pudding
1 (8 oz.) tub frozen whip-
    ped topping, thawed

1 (16 oz..) pkg. chocolate
    sandwich cookies,
    crushed
8 (9 oz.) plastic cups
gummi worms and frogs
peanuts or granola (opt.)

1. Mix milk and pudding in large bowl. Beat with a
    whisk until well blended. Let stand 5 minutes.
2. Add whipped topping and half the crushed cookies.
3. Place 1 Tb. crushed cookies in each cup. Fill cups
    3/4 full of pudding mixture. Top with remaining
    crushed cookies.
4. Chill at least 1 hour or until ready to serve.
        Decorate with: "rocks" from peanuts or granola
                or candy rocks from the candy store.
        "creatures" (gummi worms and frogs).
        "flowers" - insert a drinking straw into dirt
                cup and place a real or silk flower in straw
                to resemble a flower growing in the dirt.
    Use orange pudding at Halloween.

These can also be made in individual serving size
flower pots for a party with a garden theme.

"Sand Buckets"

Use vanilla or butterscotch pudding / vanilla cookies.
Put gummi fish in the sand buckets.

♥ WRAPPING: Wrap each dirt cup in clear plastic
wrap and tie with raffia or curling ribbon.

♥ BAKE SALES: Keep refrigerated as long as
possible. Good for concession stands wtih refrigerators.

♥ BIRTHDAY PARTIES: Prepare one dirt cup in a
large flowerpot. Place a bud vase in center and stick
in a bunch of flowers. This can be on the table for the
entire time and you can surprise children (and adults)
by removing the flowers and serving the"dirt".

Candy Apples

6 small apples
6 craft sticks
1 1/3 cups sugar

2 cups light corn syrup
1/4 tsp. red food coloring

1. Wash apples and remove stems. Insert sticks. Set aside. Place wax paper on a baking sheet and spray with cooking spray.
2. Combine sugar, corn syrup and red food coloring in top of double boiler. Cook over low heat, stirring constantly for 4 minutes. Cover and simmer 8 more minutes.
3. Uncover and cook to 300° on candy thermometer. (Hard crack stage.)
4. Turn off heat and quickly dunk each apple into hot syrup. Drip excess syrup into pan. Place on prepared baking sheet to cool.

Caramel Marshmallow Apples

5 to 6 small apples
5 to 6 craft sticks
1 (14 oz.) pkg. caramels, unwrapped

1 cup mini marshmallows
1 Tb. water

1. Wash apples and remove stems. Insert sticks. Set aside. Place wax paper on a baking sheet and spray with cooking spray.
2. Combine caramels, marshmallows and water in medium pan. Cook over medium heat, stirring constantly, until caramels melt. Remove from heat and cool slightly.
3. Dip in caramel mixture and place on prepared baking sheet. Refrigerate until firm.

Can drizzle with melted chocolate or roll in chopped nuts before refrigerating.

♥ WRAPPING: Wrap in plastic wrap or colored cellophane and tie with raffia or curling ribbon.

♥ BAKE SALES: Good for Halloween carnivals and concession stands.

Decorated Caramel Apples

5 small apples
5 craft sticks

1 (14 oz.) pkg. caramels, unwrapped
2 Tb. water

Decorations: candy melting disks, mini chocolate chips, candy corn, chopped nuts, assorted candies.

1. Wash apples and remove stems. Insert sticks. Set aside. Place wax paper on a baking sheet and spray with cooking spray.
2. Combine caramels and water in top of double boiler. Bring water to a boil. Reduce heat and cook until caramels melt, stirring often. Remove from heat.
3. Dip apples in caramel mixture. covering completely. Place apples on prepared baking sheet to cool.
4. These can be eaten as is or decorated by drizzling with melted chocolate, sprinkling with chopped nuts or mini chocolate chips. Kids can make designs or faces on the apples by attaching candies to the caramel before it sets.

Buy sheets of caramel (in the produce department) in the fall of the year and use them instead of melting caramels. Follow the directions with the caramel sheets.

♥ **WRAPPING:** Wrap in plastic wrap or colored cellophane and tie with raffia or curling ribbon.

♥ **BAKE SALES:** Good for Halloween carnivals, fall bake sales and concession stands.

Crispy Treats

1/2 stick margarine   5 cups crisp rice cereal
40 large marshmallows

1. Place margarine and marshmallows in large microsafe dish. Micro on high 1 minute at a time, stirring after each, until marshmallows are melted.
2. Place cereal in large bowl and pour marshmallow mixture over. Mix well. Work with this while it is still warm. Butter or spray your hands to work with mixture.
3. Use in recipes below and on facing page.

Crispy Treat Candy Canes

1. Use recipe above. Shape warm mixture into candy cane shapes.
2. While treats are sticky press crushed hard peppermint candies over the cane shapes.
4. Wrap in clear plastic wrap (or sandwich bags). Tie a red bow around the cane.

Crispy Treat Trees

1. Use recipe above. Add green food coloring to marshmallow mixture while it is cooking.
2. Shape warm mixture into cone shapes.
3. Decorate with small candies for ornaments.

♥ WRAPPING: Wrap in plastic wrap or sandwich bags. Tie a bow around the shaped or molded treats.

♥ BAKE SALES: Perennially popular at bake sales and concession stands.

♥ BIRTHDAY PARTIES: Treats can be molded in shapes to suit the occasion or theme.

Crispy Treat Snowmen

1. Use recipe for Crispy Treats on facing page.
   Shape warm mixture into balls (golf or tennis size).
2. Stack 2 balls together while sticky.
3. Decorate with candies for buttons, mini chocolate
   chips for eyes and a red string licorice for a scarf.

Crispy Treat Super Kiss

1. Use recipe for Crispy Treats on facing page.
   Press warm mixture firmly into a sprayed funnel.
2. Remove from funnel onto wax paper. Allow to set up.
   It will have the shape of a candy kiss.
3. Leave it as is or dip in melted chocolate. (Can add 1/2
   cup chocolate chips to marshmallow mixture while
   cooking to add some chocolate color and flavor.)

♥ WRAPPING: Wrap in plastic wrap or a sandwich
bag. Tie a bow around the shaped or molded treats.

♥ BAKE SALES: Perennially popular at bake sales
and concession stands.

♥ BIRTHDAY PARTIES: Treats can be molded in
shapes to suit the occasion or theme.

Molded Crispy Treats

There are commercial molds available at crafts
stores that can be used for shaping crispy treats.
(Be sure what you buy is meant for food.)

These come in many animal and other popular
shapes. They make cute shaped crispy treats very
quickly.

Cookbook Cupboard sells these molds. If you can't
find them in your area, send a note to the address on
the copyright page in this book asking for an order
blank for the crispy molds.

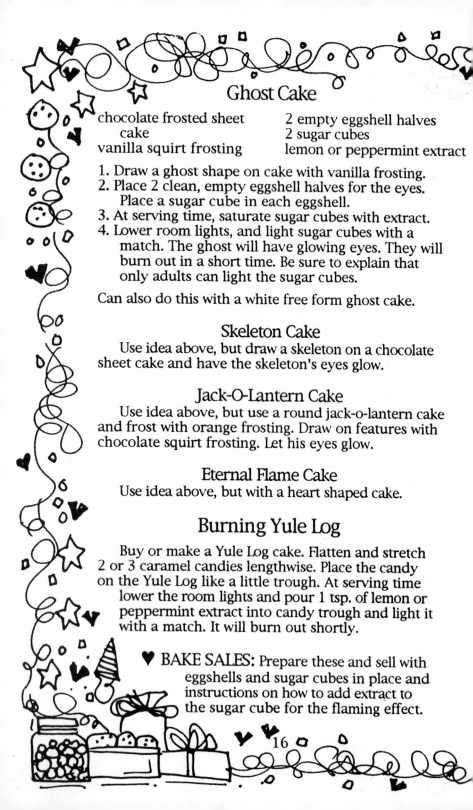

Ghost Cake

chocolate frosted sheet
   cake
vanilla squirt frosting

2 empty eggshell halves
2 sugar cubes
lemon or peppermint extract

1. Draw a ghost shape on cake with vanilla frosting.
2. Place 2 clean, empty eggshell halves for the eyes. Place a sugar cube in each eggshell.
3. At serving time, saturate sugar cubes with extract.
4. Lower room lights, and light sugar cubes with a match. The ghost will have glowing eyes. They will burn out in a short time. Be sure to explain that only adults can light the sugar cubes.

Can also do this with a white free form ghost cake.

Skeleton Cake

Use idea above, but draw a skeleton on a chocolate sheet cake and have the skeleton's eyes glow.

Jack-O-Lantern Cake

Use idea above, but use a round jack-o-lantern cake and frost with orange frosting. Draw on features with chocolate squirt frosting. Let his eyes glow.

Eternal Flame Cake

Use idea above, but with a heart shaped cake.

Burning Yule Log

Buy or make a Yule Log cake. Flatten and stretch 2 or 3 caramel candies lengthwise. Place the candy on the Yule Log like a little trough. At serving time lower the room lights and pour 1 tsp. of lemon or peppermint extract into candy trough and light it with a match. It will burn out shortly.

♥ BAKE SALES: Prepare these and sell with eggshells and sugar cubes in place and instructions on how to add extract to the sugar cube for the flaming effect.

16

Halloween Hands

popped corn
clear food handler's
   gloves (restaurant
   supply store)
candy corn

rubber bands
orange and black
   curling ribbon
plastic spider rings

1. Place 3 pieces of candy corn in each glove finger.
2. Fill gloves with popcorn. Close with rubber bands.
3. Tie ribbons over rubber bands.
4. Put a spider ring on one finger of each glove.

Ghost Lollipops

ball shaped lollipops
black ribbon

white Kleenex
black marking pen

1. Cover lollipop with Kleenex.
2. Tie Kleenex on lollipop with black ribbon.
3. Make 2 eyes on Kleenex with black marking pen.

♥ BAKE SALES: Simple for a Halloween carnival.

♥ BIRTHDAY PARTIES: Good Halloween party favors or trick or treat treats.

Halloween Ice Ring

1. Fill a ring mold with ginger ale, apple juice or colored water.
2. Drop in gummi worms candies. Freeze.
3. Unmold and float in a punch bowl filled with punch or ginger ale.

Do in ice cube trays for "worm" ice cubes.

Ghost Chocolate Pie

1. Use marshmallow creme to make a free form ghost on top of a homemade or purchased chocolate pie. Chill pie first.
2. Add chocolate chips or Red Hots for eyes.

17

Cookie Cutter Cakes

1 purchased frozen
    pound cake, thawed
Icing: 2 1/4 cups pow-
    dered sugar
2 Tb. light corn syrup

1 Tb. margarine, melted
3 Tb. water
1/4 tsp. vanilla
food coloring (opt.)

1. Slice pound cake into 1/2" thick slices.
2. Cut shapes from cake slices with metal outline cookie
    cutters.
3. Mix icing ingredients in a medium bowl.
4. Place cake cut-outs on a rack over a baking sheet to
    catch icing drips.
5. Spoon icing over cake. Leave on rack until icing sets.

These can be decorated with purchased cake decors in seasonal shapes. Put a Christmas tree decor on a Christmas tree cake, an Easter bunny decor on a bunny cake, flower decors on any shape cake. Add decors before icing sets.

These can be decorated with candied violets (buy at gourmet shops) or with edible flowers (produce dept. of larger grocery stores).

♥ **WRAPPING:** Package 6 of these in a clear deli container with colored tissue paper. Tie with curling ribbons that coordinate in color with the cakes. You can also tie on a cookie cutter of the shape you used to cut the cakes.

♥ **BAKE SALES:** Package as described above.

♥ **BIRTHDAY PARTIES:** These are bite sized cakes - fun for little children or in a dessert tray assortment for adults.

18

Ice Cream Cone Clowns

scoops of ice cream
3" round cookies
pointed ice cream cones

tube of squirt frosting
maraschino cherries
chocolate chips
red string licorice

1. Place a scoop of ice cream into each cookie.
2. Place cone at an angle on top of ice cream as a "clown hat".
3. Place on baking sheet and freeze until hard.
4. Squirt frosting around where ice cream joins cookie to make a clown collar.
5. Squirt frosting on ice cream at edge of cone to make "hair". Squirt dabs of frosting up cone and on point of cone for decorations.
6. Make face on ice cream with chocolate chips for eyes, cherries for nose and licorice for mouth.

   These can be wrapped in foil or placed in freezer bags and frozen for several days.

Caterpillar Cake

1. Arrange 12 purchased "Snowball" cupcakes on a baking sheet to form the body of a wiggly caterpillar.
2. Attach red or black string licorice to sides of each cupcake for legs.
3. Use 2 gumdrops for eyes and 2 pipe cleaners topped with gumdrops for antenna.

♥ BIRTHDAY PARTIES: Let your child help make this. Easy to serve because each of 12 children could have one of the cupcakes.

Marshmallows with Chocolate "Hats"

milk chocolate chips
large marshmallows

decorations such as
   cherries, nuts, silver
   candy balls, colored
   sprinkles

1. Spread a sheet of waxed paper on a baking sheet.
2. Melt chocolate chips over barely simmering water in top of double boiler.
3. Drop a heaping teaspoon of melted chocolate onto waxed paper. Spread into a circle a little larger than marshmallow. Place a marshmallow into chocolate.
4. Top marshmallow with more melted chocolate (like a hat).
5. Decorate the "hat" with some of the decorations mentioned in the ingredients.
6. Chill until chocolate has set. Remove from waxed paper with a spatula.

Springtime: Use colored marshmallows and pastel decorations for springtime occasions.

Marshmallow Bunnies

1. Drop a heaping teaspoon of melted chocolate (or white or pastel candy melting disks) onto waxed paper. Spread into a circle a little larger than a marshmallow bunny or chick.
2. Place the bunny into the melted chocolate.
3. Sprinkle chocolate with colored sprinkles or green-tinted coconut to represent grass.

♥ **WRAPPING:** Place in paper cupcake liners inside an egg carton.

♥ **BAKE SALES:** Sell dozens in egg cartons.

Chocolate Dipped Marshmallows

Melt milk chocolate or any color candy disks over barely simmering water in a double boiler.

Insert a craft stick into a large marshmallow and cover with melted chocolate. Sprinkle with colored or chocolate sprinkles.

Stand in a juice glass and place in refrigerator to set.

♥ WRAPPING: Wrap in plastic wrap and tie with curling ribbon at the top of the stick.

Chocolate Dipped Strawberries

1 basket large strawberries
   (with stems if possible)
foil cupcake liners

8 oz. semisweet choc-
   olate squares

1. Rinse strawberries and pat dry.
2. Melt chocolate over barely simmering water in double boiler. Stir until smooth.
3. Hold each strawberry by its stem or a toothpick. Tilt pan and use spoon to coat each berry with chocolate. Hold each berry upside down to catch drips.
4. Place berries in cupcake liners or in a foil lined pan.
5. Chill until firm. Serve at room temperature.

Variations:

Dip some strawberries in white candy coating and some in chocolate.

Dip each berry first in one color and when it has chilled, redip in the other color. Dip only part way up in the second color so both colors show.

♥ WRAPPING: Place in a foam egg carton with tissue paper for easy carrying. Cut egg carton in half to hold 6 strawberries.

Fortune Cake

1 frosted, decorated cake	index cards
narrow curling ribbon	foil

1. Cut index cards into 12 strips, 2" x 1/2" each. Write fortunes on each strip.
2. Cover fortunes tightly with foil. Punch a hole near the end of each strip.
3. Tie a bow through hole with curling ribbon. Curl ends of ribbon. Add a small silk flower if you like.
4. Gently push each fortune into the sides of the cake. The ribbons will show where the fortunes are and will decorate the cake. Place them evenly so each piece of cake will have a fortune.

Fortune Cupcakes

Fortunes can also be placed in the top of individual cupcakes for a birthday party or a bake sale.

♥ BAKE SALES: Place this cake in a deli cake pan with a clear cover. Be sure and label it "Fortune Cake" and explain that each person is to pull out the fortune by the ribbon before eating his piece of cake. Fortune Cupcakes are also good for bakes sales or concession stands.

♥ BIRTHDAY PARTIES: Also good for adult parties.

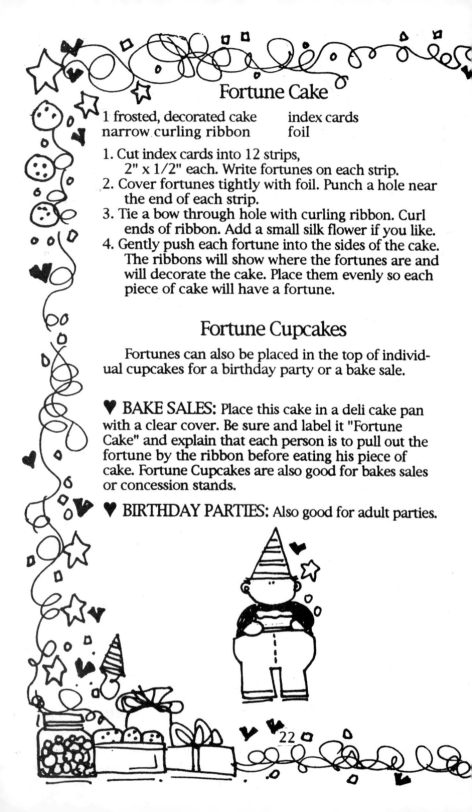

Fortune Easter Eggs

1. Make a small hole with a needle on one end of a raw egg and a larger hole on the other end. Use needle to puncture egg yolk. Blow through the small hole over a bowl to catch the egg.
2. Rinse the eggshells very well and drain.
3. Decorate the eggs any way you like.
4. Write "fortunes" on little strips of paper. Roll up the strip tightly and push into egg through the large hole.

♥ WRAPPING: Place on colored tissue in egg cartons.

♥ BAKE SALES: Add a Fortune Egg to another bake sale item as an added attraction.

♥ BIRTHDAY PARTIES: Fun for a birthday party around Easter. Stack the eggs in a bowl as a centerpiece on a nest of Easter grass.

Easter Basket Cupcakes

1. Bake your favorite cupcake recipe in foil liners. Cool.
2. Frost top with vanilla frosting. Make an indentation in frosting to make a "nest".
3. Sprinkle cupcake with green tinted coconut (put coconut in a jar and add 2 to 3 drops each green food coloring and water - put lid on jar and shake).
4. Top with small Easter candies.
5. Insert a pastel pipe cleaner to represent basket handle. Tie (or hot glue) a small bow on pipe cleaner.

Fancy Peanut Butter Sandwich Cookies

candy melting disks (crafts or baking supply stores), your choice of colors

Ritz Crackers or vanilla wafers
peanuts butter
colored sprinkles

1. Melt candy disks in double boiler.
2. Make a "sandwich" by spreading peanut butter between 2 crackers.
3. Dip sandwiches in melted candy. (It is easier to dip if candy is placed in small deep container like a measuring cup.) Stand in a juice glass and refrigerate until set.
4. Decorate with sprinkles while candy is still wet.

If you wish, you can insert a craft stick in each sandwich.

Sprinkle with Christmas sprinkles, pastel sprinkles, silver or gold sprinkles.

Oreo Cookie Pops

Insert a craft stick in an Oreo cookie. Dip cookie in melted milk chocolate chips. Stand in a juice glass and refrigerate until set. Decorate with colored sprinkles before chocolate sets, if desired.

♥ WRAPPING: Wrap finished cookies with colored cellophane. Tie a bow of curling ribbon to hold cellophane in place.

♥ BAKE SALES: Good in a basket of goodies.

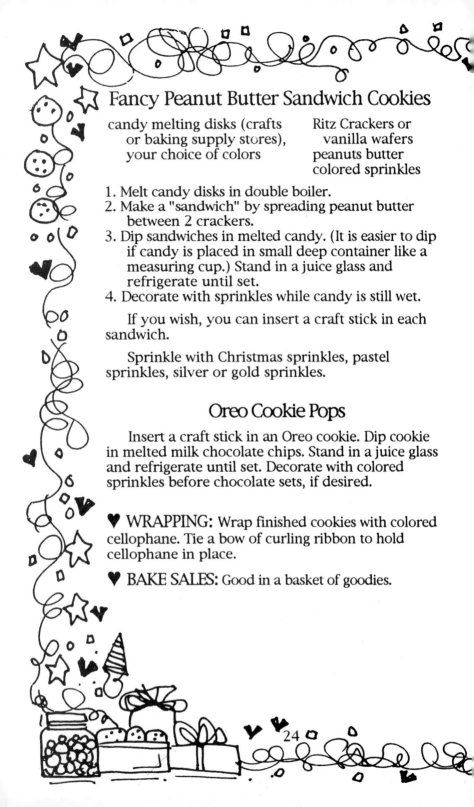

Face Cookies on a Stick

1. Shape cookie dough into 1" balls. Use refrigerated dairy case cookie dough or homemade sugar cookie dough.
2. Dip a flat bottom glass in sugar and flatten each ball. Insert a craft stick in each.
3. Bake according to pkg. directions or recipe directions.
4. Cool completely on baking sheet. Remove carefully with a spatula.
5. Decorate with candies and squirt frosting to resemble faces or any decoration you like. Use assorted candies and nuts. Glue on with squirt frosting or corn syrup.

♥ WRAPPING: Wrap in plastic wrap (or sandwich bags) and tie with multi-colored curling ribbons.

♥ BIRTHDAY PARTIES: Make a face cookie to resemble each guest. Tie on a tag with each name on it.

Circus Parade

1. Sandwich two vanilla wafers with purchased frosting.
2. Place a dab of frosting on top and stand up an animal cracker.
3. Line the cookies up to make a parade.

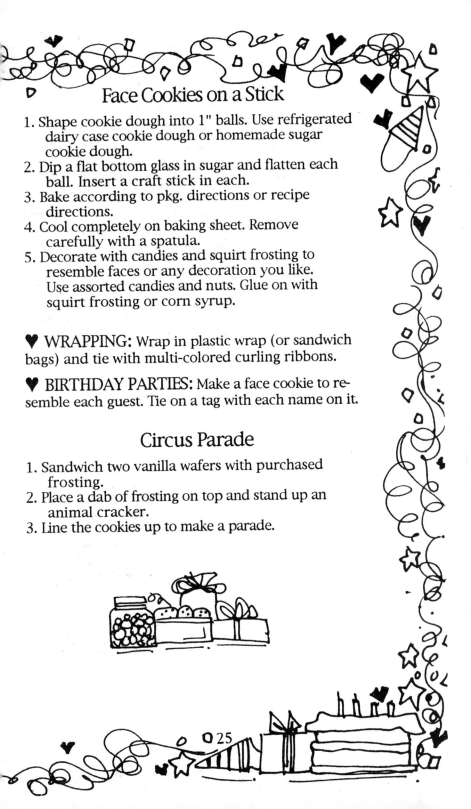

Flying Saucer Cookies

2 sticks margarine
1 cup peanut butter
1 cup sugar
1 cup packed brown sugar
2 eggs

1 1/4 cups flour
1 tsp. baking soda
1/2 tsp. salt
2 1/4 cups quick oats
1 cup M and M's candies

1. Place margarine, peanut butter and sugar in large bowl. Mix with electric mixer until light and fluffy.
2. Add eggs and mix slightly.
3. Mix flour, soda, salt and oats in another bowl and blend with a whisk.
4. Add dry ingredients to creamed mixture. Mix until well blended. Stir in 2/3 cup candies.
5. Drop by 1/3 cup measures onto sprayed nonstick baking sheet. Bake at 350 for 18 to 20 minutes. Press remaining candies onto cookies. Cool 3 to 4 minutes on baking sheet. Remove to rack to finish cooling.

♥ BAKE SALES: Perennially popular at bake sales and concession stands.

26

Holiday Pretzels

1. Dip large stick or knot pretzels in melted candy coating (use a color of candy coating to match the holiday or the occasion).
2. Sprinkle with mini holiday sprinkles (mini bunnies, mini hearts - these are available at holiday time with the cake decors in the grocery store).
3. Place on wax paper lined baking sheet and refrigerate until firm.

♥ **WRAPPING:** Place a dozen of these in a small white box lined with holiday colored tissue.

♥ **BAKE SALES:** Good in a basket of goodies.

♥ **BIRTHDAY PARTIES:** Easy to do these to match the theme or occasion.

Hamburger Cookies

coconut
food coloring
purchased vanilla frosting
vanilla wafers

round chocolate mint candies
light corn syrup
sesame seeds

1. Color coconut with green food coloring.
2. Spread a little vanilla frosting on bottom of one vanilla wafer. Top with some green coconut to be lettuce.
3. Top coconut with candy mint. Spread mint with more vanilla frosting (or tint it yellow to be mustard)
4. Top with another vanilla wafer.
5. Brush top lightly with corn syrup and sprinkle with sesame seeds.

Chocolate Cut-Outs

1 (12 oz.) pkg. semisweet
   chocolate chips
2/3 cup sweetened con-
   densed milk

1/4 tsp. salt
1 tsp. vanilla (opt.)

1. Place a large sheet of foil into a 9" square pan with edges hanging over pan.
2. Melt chocolate chips, milk and salt in small pan over very low heat, stirring constantly. Remove from heat as soon as it is nearly melted. Add vanilla.
3. Spread into prepared pan and refrigerate 1 hour or until firm.
4. Lift out candy by foil. Place candy side down on cutting board and remove foil.
5. Cut by pressing metal outline cookie cutters into chocolate with the heel of your hand. Lift out and push candy out with your thumb. If candy is too hard to handle, let it set out a few minutes. If it is too soft to handle, chill 15 minutes. Lift cut outs with a spatula.

♥ WRAPPING: Place several of these in a small colorful Chinese take out box (craft stores, Container Store) with colored tissue. Tie on a cookie cutter like the one used for the cut-outs.

♥ BIRTHDAY PARTIES: Arrange these on a tray with Cookie Cutter Cakes (pg. 18) and Ice Cream Cut-Outs (pg. 30).

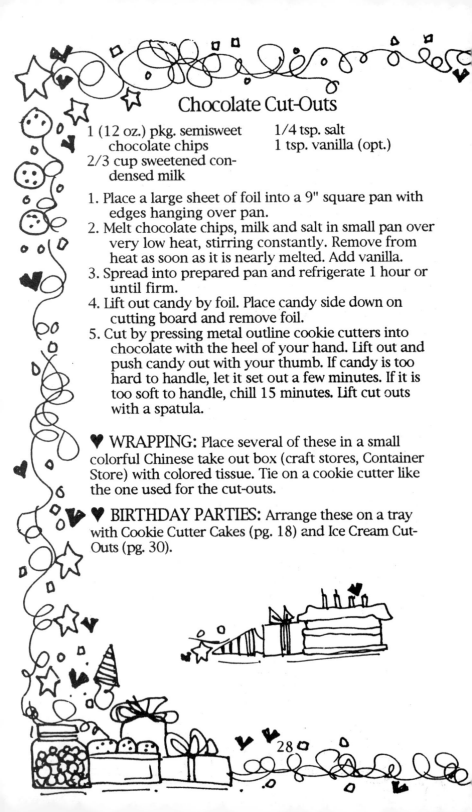

Chocolate Peanut Butter Cut-Outs

1 stick margarine
1 cup graham cracker
   crumbs (buy crumbs)
2 cups peanut butter,
   smooth or chunky

1/2 cup packed brown sugar
2 1/2 cups powdered sugar
1 (12 oz.) pkg. semisweet chocolate chips

1. Melt margarine in microwave.
2. Place all ingredients except chocolate chips in large bowl. Add melted margarine. Mix until well blended. Mixture will be sticky.
3. Spread evenly onto a baking sheet (wetting your hands will help spread mixture).
4. Melt chocolate chips and spread immediately over peanut butter layer.
5. Chill 1 hour. Remove from refrigerator. Let stand at room temperature 10 minutes.
6. Cut into shapes with metal outline cookie cutters. Remove from sheet with spatula. Press out candy with your thumb.

These taste like peanut butter cups.

♥ BAKE SALES: Good in a basket of goodies. Package a few together for sale at concession stands.

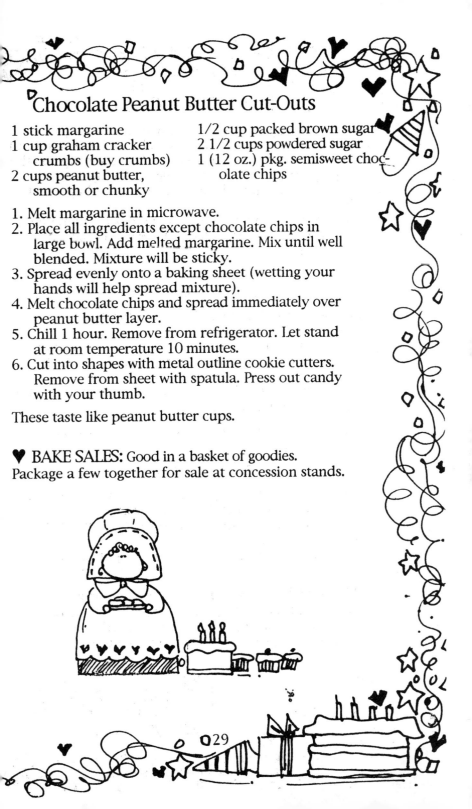

Candy in a Cookie Cutter

Plan on giving a cookie cutter with each candy. Buy metal outline cookie cutters of all one shape or several shapes appropriate to the occasion. Make the recipe on the facing page, but instead of pressing the candy out with your thumb, leave it in the cookie cutter. It is important for the candy to be the same thickness as the cookie cutter. Can sprinkle with colored sprinkles before candy sets up (before cutting).

Ice Cream Cut-Outs

1. Make a layer of ice cream 1/2" thick in a flat pan. Freeze until hard.
2. Press metal outline cookie cutters into the ice cream with the heel of your hand for pressure. Push out ice cream with your thumb.
3. Store in plastic freezer container, separating layers with wax paper, until needed.

Can decorate with candy sprinkles before freezing.

Pound Cake Cut-Outs

1. Slice purchased frozen pound cake into slices the same thickness as your metal outline cookie cutters.
2. Cut shapes with cookie cutters. Serve with matching ice cream cut-outs (above).
3. Squirt designs on cake cut-outs with squirt frosting.

♥ BIRTHDAY PARTIES: Serve matching ice cream and cake cut-outs for parties for little kids. They will enjoy the small size, the cute shapes and choosing the ones they want off a tray.

30

Heart Shaped Cake
(without a special pan)

1. Bake your cake recipe in one 9" round cake pan and one 9" square pan.
2. Place the square cake into a diamond shape on a large serving plate.
3. Cut round cake in half and place each half next to top left side and right side of diamond. You may need to trim the corners to line up the pieces.

   If you need help visualizing this, cut out a 9" circle and a 9" square out of paper to see how they fit together.

Heart Shaped Cupcakes
(without a special pan)

1. Use your favorite cake recipe to make cupcakes. Place paper baking cups in muffin tins. Put a marble or small ball of foil in each cup between paper liner and pan. This makes a heart shaped mold.
2. Pour in cake batter and bake as usual. Fill only half full or you will not have the heart shaped ffect.
3. Decorate by squirting frosting around the top to accent the heart shape. Put a candy "I Love You" heart on top.

31

Index